ABOUT THE AUTHOR

Sharena Lee Satti is a Poet, Spoken v
shop facilitator, she is female advocate for women, pushing the
boundaries and always campaigning for their voices to be heard
in society. Since sharena release of She, her first published
collection with The Verve back in November 2020 at the midst of
the pandemic, Sharena is a real advocate for encouraging poetry
and passionately supporting the art form in her City of Bradford and beyond. She believes in the power of poetry and works
extremely hard within her community and online to make sure
poetry is accessible for all. This has seen her nominated for the
National Diversity award 2022, One of the 21' of 2021 creatives
most likely to make an impact on Bradfords cultural scene and
The British Indian awards 2020, her work is seen locally and
nationally amongst schools and Universities, working with
organisations and delivering community projects. Most
recently working with Maya Productions, Hospice UK, Women
Zone, Bradford Literature festival, Huddersfield literature
festival, Sangam festival. Abda Khan, The Leap, Bradford
Libraries, Leeds Play House.

Sharena Lee Satti
Shhhhhhhh

VERVE
POETRY PRESS
BIRMINGHAM

PUBLISHED BY VERVE POETRY PRESS
https://vervepoetrypress.com
mail@vervepoetrypress.com

All rights reserved
© 2023 Sharena Lee Satti

The right of Sharena Lee Satti to be identified as author of this work has been asserted in accordance with section 77 of the Copyright, Designs and Patents Act 1988.

No part of this work may be reproduced, stored or transmitted in any form or by any means, graphic, electronic, recorded or mechanical, without the prior written permission of the publisher.

FIRST PUBLISHED OCT 2023

Printed and bound in the UK
by ImprintDigital, Exeter

ISBN: 978-1-913917-44-9

Cover Illustration by Marcela Diaz

*To the women and girls
of the world*

CONTENTS

Shssss	11
In her bed	12
Can I tell you a secret?	13
Rejected	15
Lulu	16
Step over her	17
I'm going to Marry you	18
Sat there	19
Lights out	21
Wake me up tomorrow	24
Born the mistake	25
Stalker	26
Rapunzel	27
Not enough for you	28
Dying to be thin	29
It's Red	30
Not Visible	32
Different Versions of you	34
I don't want a boyfriend	35
Mirror Mirror	36
Memory Loss	37
I cry with you	39
The bookstore	40

Speak your truth	41
Nothing	42
The Hand that rocks the cradle	43
You Jumped	44
In your eyes	45
Can you see?	47
Let go	49
Keeping you safe	50
Blind	51
Partition	53
A Mother's love	55
Fannie Lou Hamer	57
She (Part 2)	58
Family	59
Forbidden love	60
Feeding my soul	62
Grandparents	64
Without me	66
Christmas without you	68
Anxiety	70
My silence	72
Write	74
I'm helpless in Helping you	76
What is happiness	79
Do you have moments?	82
Me, myself and my poetry	84
Different	86

The Light of the Lantern	88
Saying no	90
Break the Bias	93
DEEDS NOT WORDS IWD	96
Faces of the present Iwd 2021	98
Embrace Equity	100

Afterword, Thankyous, Guests.

Shhhhhhhh

Shssss don't speak

No longer will she stay quiet
To please your narrative
You may find these words
Uncomfortable
They may spark emotions
You don't want to feel
Sometimes we have to scream
In order to heal
We have to share our pain
In order to breathe again
So HERE WE SHARE WITH YOU

Shssss

Hold the silence, hold the space, stay silent
Bury that grief amongst the violence
Amongst the ghosts of your presence
That's forever alive within her
Torturing her and her tongue remains
Numb to the silence, numb to her senses
Allowing the demons to escape the consequences
Whilst she carried the pain
In between her rib cage
And the dried-up blood stains
That you carved into her existence
The scars that you scraped and scraped
Till she bled and bled
The wounds that you carved
Starved a heart from feeling human
A word she disconnected from
Woman to man, woman still includes man
She was no woman of no man
Just a girl
A creation formed by his hand
By his thorns that he placed around her neck
His rose had to be protected
Never allowing his control to be distilled
It had to remain infectious
As he whispers shssss little girl
Stay silent
Her silence was sealed, her lips clenched shut
Screaming from inside
Silence as he fucked.

In her bed

The stale smell of woody cologne drenched in sweat
hit her nose well before her eyes
Could analyse what the fire of hell had in store for her
She carried the little strength she had left to
Take a step forward, her legs ached
From the lack of work breaks
And the endless walk home
She pushed opened the door
It creaked, lagging on the floor
Was this a warning before she entered
What kind of alarm was this
She wasn't prepared for this
Laid scrunched in her bed sheets
Like it was his
Smiling at her like she was his
Moving her bed sheets
That wreaked of stale piss
And his body odour
That lingered like death
And every breath that he took
made her body shrivel up
curling her toes and craving to wake up
Surely this couldn't be true
How could her Mother just let you
Lay across her bed sheets
Knowing you want her in between you
And the duvet cover that once smelt so sweet
You thought you could have her
And cover your brutal intentions with
The cloth of her sheets.

Can I tell you a secret?

She's always been afraid of the police
The boys in blue, the men in uniform that are out to protect us
Always gave her that uncomfortable vibe that she was never protected enough
They were above the law
And even she didn't trust them
She would have to unlock that door
ordered by law
"Who was she", just a child
and their sniggers and smiles
At her breasts in her white silky t-shirt
Which wasn't just the first time his eyes spoke to her chest
As they came to arrest her younger siblings
Telling her she is the good girl, always the good girl
That lives in a fire whirl of disruptive fierce winds
That poverty and crime brings
As he still talks to her chest
Their power always overpowered her
Their control never sit right with her
Even racially, being the penny in a bunch of 5ps
She had no freedom to speak anything above the emergency services
Even if it was about the truth of justice
So, whenever they visited her premises
She nervously smiled at his conversations
Whilst trying to seek validation within
She knew the rules always seemed different for her, for us
Always broken to us, never fair to us
We are told to trust
Law is law, this officer is seeking an excuse to take her brothers

to the station
But using this as an invitation to talk to her breasts
And when his eyes are removed from her chest
She felt a wave of fear hitting her hard
Like glass pieces of shards that had scattered and left her defenceless
Not acting upon her senses that leave her so senseless
He knocks at her door every other day, showing his authority
Today is another robbery and she is home alone
Bent down at the dryer pulling clothes from the machine
Wishing the glass door panels didn't show her shadow, making her seen
To the eyes that talk to her chest
Watching the movement of her breath
As it rapidly speeds, and she is visibly struggling
To breathe as her anxiety kicks in
Suffocating under the pressure of her own heart beating
Under the arrest of his eyes
You can't hide from the prey that seeks you in disguise nor those whom we are told to trust
Programmed to never challenge those above
Like we are not seen as enough
And his eyes can rest upon wherever he feels lawful
Her body his station, her breasts part of his checklist
And his sniggers and smiles are still handcuffed to her wrists
As his eyes to her chest, 25 years later and she can still see your eyes undressing a child
A police officer smiled but he was a police officer right. A good man right, all above the peasants he protects
The law he infects but he is the one dedicated to protect and serve the people.

Rejected

She turned her head away from you
 every time you wanted her attention
You stretching your vocal chords to
 strengthen the depth of your words
To get her to look in your direction
and when her eyes never gazed at yours
destruction erupted within you
It wasn't acceptable behaviour that she never saw you
You weren't of this earth to her
Yet you thought you were of worth to her
In your power tripped adult world, you wanted this girl
That didn't even look at you as human
What you were doing was child grooming
Trying to manipulate a child into wanting you
A predator trying to pursue
All that should be legally off bounds to you
But who would ever come to know
He carefully selected who he wanted to show
And because the little girl said no
He violated her, called her the names
That tormented her with pain
Way before those words of shame touched his lips
He screeched in her face 'you are fat and ugly anyway'
And she knew this to be true, but she barricaded that pain inside
Trying to hide the tears that left her eyes
And the silence that kept her lips shut tight
Holding back the fire that screamed inside
The virgin that bruised his pride, his electric ego
For defending her body and the right to say no.

Lulu

You gifted her the ocean's fragrance
With grooves engraved into its fine glass waves
That bathed the air with such delicacy
A soft gentle essence that disguised the enemy
She was your favourite, something about her innocence
And her mother's hate that made you want to mutate
That twistedness into a timeless piece of her existence
She was pure and you cashed in on her vulnerability
Handing her bank notes, that sugar cane sweetness
You wanted her to indulge in
To taste the pigment of her skin, the brownness
Oh the brownness of her ancestral roots
You wanted to digest a piece of that youth
That you would never taste again
Or that you never ever tasted
She was the same age as your own daughter
That you were not allowed to see
And she looked disgusted that you were allowed to be free
Planting bank notes in a child's hand
Unknown to her what you had planned
You were a paedophile, but she saw you as just a man
That showed a young girl to never take from a hand
That targeted her, with his gifts and smiles
That said it's okay, you never get anything
And being a child, it felt like everything to be handed
A £20 note when her mother never gave her a pound
And every safe space was no longer safe to those she was around
A child in a vulture's world, being preyed upon
Never saved upon, never saved.

Step over her

She pretended not to see
Exactly what you wanted her to see
She kept her head held up, looking up
But she could still see your flesh being
covered by his flesh, your legs
spread like a stunned piece of meat
rotting under the heat of his skin
His jeans just resting below your ankles
Your bones buried under him
Under his weight that would suffocate
Anyone else but him
He had entered in, with your permission
Poison that should have been forbidden
You were a desert flower, growing amongst the heat
That grew from within the grains of sand
You were never meant to survive on that land
You were supposed to perish, wither and die
But you watered your own roots with the tears
That you cried and you
You, you fought and survived
And here we are, here you are
Laid across the floor, like the whore
He thinks you are
What happened to the desert flower
That survived, that cried, that fought the fire to
breathe
Not to lay beneath another Man's sheets
Seeking his Love.

I'm going to Marry you

I'm going to marry you one day
Is all they would say
Each tone of the voice slightly different from the next
Like she should be pleased they see her more than just sex
She is wife material until she opens her legs

I'm going to marry you one day
Is all they would say
As she silently sat there looking away, trying to lower her gaze
But as her gaze dropped, the voices didn't stop
They became louder, till she heard every word
That bounced off the walls of her skin

I'm going to marry you one day
Is all they would say
In their heavily scented cologne
Like this was a marriage proposal left open
And she would be forced to be his prized possession
Still, saying no is an expression of acceptance

I'm going to marry you one day
And take you away from the mornings you awake
To visit the bus for school you take
I'm going to make, you, my teenage bride
Ignoring the no that she had just replied
And once again he said
I'm going to marry you one day.

Sat there

You sat there; your frail body wrapped in vulnerability that disguised the human
For the first time you looked off guard, unprotected carved into this confusion
Of helplessness of despair of knowing not a soul in this world cares
And the ones that do are just as vulnerable
She sits there, a blank canvas hiding her grief
Covered partially with her bed sheets
Rubbing her feet together, making this noise
That irritates the ears like sandpaper grinding together
It brought her comfort in some kind of way
That no one ever but her could understand
She sat amongst glass particles; windows shattered
Scattered all over her, all over the floor, the windows the doors
She refused to move, to move would be to lose everything
Being her stubborn self was her own way of self-healing
Even if that meant her sat freezing, with no windows
And a door smashed up too, her house of glass
Of worthless shattered pieces, that even the police ignored
Nothing was more alone than she
The darkness was no camouflage for her safety
But she refused to leave even though her eyes screamed "save me"
Her innocence screamed don't leave me, beg me, drag me to leave
But don't leave me, don't leave the scattered pieces of me
Shattered with this glass that clings to the floors and the walls
And everything that can be seen
She continues to sit there cloaked in walls of steel defending

her home
With darkness by her side, it brought comfort and took away the feeling of being alone.

Lights out

It's just her and the panting of her breath

As it is leaving her chest

the heaviness in between her breasts

and she knows she has to keep going

as the anxiety is growing

as it spreads throughout her bones

The eerie silent footsteps of the unknown

She knows she has to walk at a speed her heart

Is uncomfortable with

Leaving the silhouette of his, every shadow that lives

Every rustling of the leaves
every creak of wind that whistles through the trees

The danger is not looking forward it's what's behind

Knowing one wrong move could cost her her life

Even when she is trying to stay focused

She knows it's that one thing on your mind

That makes you wish could rewind

The choice of path that you've taken

Like it's your fault that he's following

The feeling of regret she keeps swallowing

Every gulp that drips down is a mouthful of fear

It's the hopelessness of knowing you're alone and he's near

You're covered in the darkness, but it's no camouflage for safety

The council lights that are switched off might have just saved her

And she is here screaming inside please don't rape me

Even her manners are still intact

Because she fears being attacked, like she is begging her thoughts

Like they can stop her from being kidnapped

But who is she fooling, she is as alone as every single star in that sky

and as helpless and as vulnerable as can be

There is not a soul around, who's going to help save her

And she is getting tired, every breath now screams out

To the clouds, to the branches on the trees, to the leaves

She is stumbling over her own feet, trying to reach some noise

To drown out this silence to obliterate the danger

But she is alone, alone with this stranger

And all the warning signs are screaming danger

As she moves faster, so does he

And there's no escaping him from her

And come tomorrow she will be, just be another name on the news

A death to another rapist on the loose

Because another man was left to abuse

A woman walking home.

Wake me up tomorrow

Stay under the covers my love
for here is where the forest grows
Where the light dances with the darkness and monsters
Are afraid of your dreams
Here is where roses paint your cheeks
and daisies clothe your skin
For here my love is a space that no one
Can get in
This is your safe haven, your creation
Those sweets that you tasted
A pure piece of your imagination
That you hold so sacred
For no one can enter the gates of your paradise
This is where your empty belly lies
Now filled with all the fruits of paradise
Leaving the warmth clinging to your insides
The sweets that sweeten your bitter afternoon
For her screams can wait outside your room
Hum dear girl, hum to the tune of your own silence
For here her violence cannot reach you
And if your doors are rattled and your windows shake
Just play dead dear girl, just play dead
If they find the entrance to the trees that weave in and out your sheets
that encased your bed
Be ready to roar girl, be ready to claw your way out
For now, you are safe, encased in the arms of your own protection
Just dream dear girl just dream.

Born the mistake

You pulled back the smoke, inhaling it deep into your lungs
Till your bones shivered, and your eyes were bloodshot red
At this point the joint you had just smoked was truly messing
with the demons in your head
But you carried on anyway, it was easier to be high
Than to acknowledge you were alive, so you picked
Up the cider too and was drinking like adults do
But you were just 11 years old
Rolling joints in rainbow coloured rizlas
Burning the black, leaving the charcoal stains on your fingers
Whilst turning drip white, her blood levels dropping
But she wasn't stopping, and her father had randomly turned up
So, she stumbled up, her feet unable to carry her body weight
She couldn't compose herself being in this state
But no one knew, how deeply you were fucking up you
The 11-year-old you, just 11 years old, who knew
How to block out her life listening to nightlife lady
Thinking of a life beyond her years
that she never believed she would see
because her time was filled with this ghosted slavery
Chained to her environment, and not a soul could see
How dangerously the storm brewed around her
Because the damaged kids were just as damaged as her
How was she ever meant to survive?
When the womb that carried her, rejected her life
And no other soul sought to harmonise the demons she couldn't
escape
So, she blocked out what she blocked out
Born the mistake.

Stalker

When she stops being her
Don't ignore
When she stops being her
Something is wrong
Something is going on
She awakes just before the breaking of dawn
When pink streaks warm the cheeks of the sky
She tiptoes out of her bedroom, down the steps
To trip the electricity switch
A reset that was caused by a technical glitch
And the alarm will not alarm her
She pauses and then breathes
Knowing today the bus will leave without her
She seeks comfort in this and her anxiety
Flows back through her body
Into the streams of her blood
And It sits there, knowing come tomorrow
She can't trip the switch and will have to take the bus
And he will be waiting there for her
For her innocence provokes his demons that stir
When he sees her
When she stands in her uniform clutching her school bag
It's when he silently attacks, getting closer to her
Moving in next to her, she can smell his breath
Engraving his perverse desires onto her skin
Every day he's stalking and everyday no one is noticing
Her changing, her hiding away, not wanting to live another day
No one sees her, who would believe her anyway.

Rapunzel

A black flowing river of her, a cloak of darkness
That stunned the light
Every lock of her, every strand that wrapped around her whole being
Was the life of her, the light of her
The radiance of the universe born within her
Every whisper of that darkness was sacred
But It couldn't protect her from her mother's hatred
Rapunzel was told to stand still
And the light shining in from the window
Painted the kitchen in hues of orange and yellow
And it caught her completely off guard
Till in came the blow that hit her hard
She wasn't standing still, the rule was not to move
and she had to prove her power
Her eyes were forbidden to see
The hair falling to her knees
Like autumn leaves it fell
And it didn't stop falling
She wanted to cling to it, to hold its softness
To wrap it around her and smell its sweet fragrance
Just one last time
For she will never bathe in her river of darkness
That you took from her
When you cut every piece of her hair
Till only fine grains were left visible
You wanted her to feel the misery
Of being miserable
Trapped in a world of you
Her ugliness pleased you, and she had to live to please you.

Not enough for you

She was too white for you; her flesh didn't paint your canvas in colour
She couldn't camouflage into your darkness
She was too light, too white to fit into your brownness
She didn't bow to your feet, or cut up her chapati
How all the others did, she preferred to nibble and dip
Savouring the taste on her lips and just pausing
She would hold her chapati with two hands
As the butter dripped it was in this moment that she loved
For this second, she would stop breathing
And breathe in all that her grandmother had crafted
For in this moment, she was accepted for being her
Never was she too white for her grandmother's love
Just the judgement of every other
She was too brown for you, her colour diluted into your whiteness
And the stains horrified you
She was the dirt that belonged to the side pavements
That you avoided when it rained when the storm came
Because it made you dirty, reminded you too much of the Earth existed in her and that pained you
She was too brown for you, a paki to you
What did she ever do, to spark the hatred in you
She wasn't enough of anything to you and her existence
Caused division and wars within herself
Rejected by everything other than the land and the sky
For the pigments of her skin were just perfectly right for
the evening sunset, every shade of her lived in that sky falling
In that light leaving, in that darkness drawing closer into her
She wasn't too brown for the sunset or too white for the Sunrise.

Dying to be thin

The ripped red lines that creased the back of your legs
Looked more aggressive today
So, she ripped of her skirt and wrapped her skin
Into your cloth of insecurity
At least there no one could see, how deeply
Your stretched skin hurt you
How it pained you to look into the mirror
And see that reflection of her looking at you
She always pointed out that you were never good enough
To wear the clothes like the others
The thin strapped dresses that bathed your body
Like an ocean, that wrapped around it like the sea
For your body was too much for a child as young as she
She forbid her body the fuel that it needed
To slow its growth but instead it bled and kept on bleeding
She hated the taste of hunger, yet she knew it was the prize of acceptance
To starve until her intestines roared at her, gripping at her insides
Not to eat is to die, but today she's looking skinny so it's alright
Her bones spoke to her, told her they looked beautiful, when they protrude
From her skin
When she looks incredibly thin, and everything screams that
she's is not eating, and the mirror keeps feeding
Her stomach the nutrients she needs
The distorted image she sees that controls
What she believes is her, in that mirror
So, she starves herself slim and the times her lips get to
taste anything is always followed by the bitter metallic
taste of the contents from her stomach.

It's Red

She knew that the red stream would run
From the wild acres of her insides
That bled into clots from cells that
Her body had not yet fertilised
You humbled her in ways that only pain can
When her ovaries are pulsing
And she is squeezing her legs tight shut
To ease the pulsing that amplifies both the pain and her wanting
The ghost of tenderness to soothe the inside of her
Why does her body always seek pain and pleasure together
It was always red's fault, that stream that made her bleed
A tsunami of torrential rain that pooled in-between her thighs
And she lied when she smiled and pretending to the world
That she had everything under control
Nothing could control the fire that
Was burning within her, a rage she couldn't contain
And a waterfall that refused to flow gently
Both sending her emotions into a sky diving wave
Of electricity, a strike of thunder
Channelling right through her body at speed
When she has to compose herself, even when
The pain is knocking her off her feet
She has to breathe and allow the red
To flow through her, the aches, the twists of
Her insides, the bloating, the emotional
Wreckage that's left, but red will continue to flow
And she will continue to rest her smile upon her dimpled cheeks when that pain grows
If you had stayed would things have been different?
Would she have come to love her own, the only way red flows?

Under a full moon the river runs red
Gripping at her ovaries, another layer of her she sheds.

Not Visible

Gravity clings to her insides
An anchor docking at sea
But she, can barely breathe
She was gasping for breath
Clinging on at the edge of death
And her pain was refusing to leave
Her screams echoed amongst the blowing breeze
and her autumn eyes pleaded
With every oxygen particle floating around her
Desperate to feel the relief
The comfort of just being able to breathe
Her deafening screams were internalised
and her suffering was buried under the invisible gagged cloth
that was forced around her mouth
Her pain sought comfort from the walls of her uterus
From the slowing beats of her heart
From the ancestral whispers of the umbilical cord
Because her own voice was being ignored
She was told to leave, the birth of her seed will not be born today
Her own voice was cast aside, rammed back inside within her
You silenced her, you made her question her own body, her own pain
Like this was a mistake, she cannot recognise when her own body
Is screaming out in a way
That displeases your medical terms for "She is in labour"
There was no relief in your clinic for sympathy
So, you sent her away, told her to sleep off her pain
Breathe it away, for only the wind would acknowledge her suffering
And that deathly feeling she was mothering
That burning of hell, the flames of fire the brink of death
Cradling her stomach, trying to gasp for breath

Knowing she can feel the head crowning in-between her legs
But once again, you dismissed her pain
So, she managed to escape the bathroom, even crawl down the steps
But she wasn't prepared for what was to happen next
Her body was a raging inferno, and all she could do was allow it to burn
Breathing through the flames, the long breathes of hot air
But who would be to blame for the lack of her care
Her legs now shivering uncontrollably, her body
Jolting in movements only her body can explain
She was told she wasn't in labour
Her face didn't express her pain
And here she was earthing her own seed
She was told she shouldn't believe
In her own pain, told to silence that voice
Like she had a choice to silence that suffering.

(Never silence that for nothing).

Different Versions of you

She walked upon the same path
watching the light fall into darkness
And the darkness fade into the light
She always paused at the red streaks of romance
that smeared across the sky
Before the darkness cloaked her vision
and wrapped its existence around her whole being
It fulfilled a part of her, that was unreachable
even for the flash of time it existed
She had walked many steps upon the same route
walking along the same cobbled path
Kicking the same dust from under her feet
and watching as the same ripples pooled into rings of
vibrational energy
The rings never changed their sequency, they always formed in the
Exact same way
From the depth of blue, a message only she knew how to interpret
She walked this path several times or more
Shedding free different layers of her, peeling back the skin
That once built a fortress around her
Is now no more than a dead leaf that is crushed under her feet
For she walks now, with a clearer vision
Her open wounded heart no longer hidden
She had indeed exhausted this route, this path, her shoes
No longer hiding under the umbrella of her abuse
For this route was forever meeting different versions of her
Even when the sky changed its face and the seasons crumbled
Under the burning rays of the sun
This path cleared her ashes that she has arisen daily from
No longer the same She, on the path she walked along.

I don't want a boyfriend

She watched men crush the lives of her love, around her
Every day a new scar, embedded deep into her heart
And she had to remain silent, like the fullness of the silence
That remains silent and doesn't allow you to speak
She stayed weak for her to be strong but her strong
Was blinded with a love that didn't acknowledge the wrong
She just couldn't see anything in between
Other than the men she thought she loved
Those she blindly trusted, until everything became nothing
And nothing pierced its way into everything she owned
Until nothing was all she homed
A house of emptiness, pieces of carpet left, a leg of a table
A piece of cable that he forgot to take too
All the men in her life gained from her life
While she struggled to stay alive and the other girls
Teased the younger one, she must be gay
Or a lesbian right
She's not got a boyfriend, she never goes near the boys
Even when they signal and make some noise
She walked with a lowered gaze trying to camouflage into the light
Into the space that awakens the difference between her
And the other girls that crave that attention
She once secretly wanted to be loved but then realised
Men don't love, they fuck, and they destroy happiness too
So, she stayed away from boys because she'd seen the destruction of what they do
So, she remained untouched whilst cursed for not wanting to be touched
To protect her heart from being crushed, she remained unloved
By a selfish society that forces young girls to love
She didn't want a boyfriend.

Mirror Mirror

You look at her and give her daily updates
At how she's aged, at how her hair is out of place
You make her want to hide her face from the world
Because she is not a beautiful girl
And the world only acknowledges her when
Her eyelashes are full and her nails
cost her more than her mum's weekly shopping
but it doesn't matter because it's beauty or nothing
She filters everything because beauty is a lie
And she chooses to hide behind all that makes her Instagram worthy
The image she sees is an image she grieves
One that displeases her, that makes her question her weight
And now she feels guilty, looking at the food portion on her plate
Your glass showed her a wave, that bathed in her skin
That triggered an alarm, that she silenced
That she secretly tries to disguise, the body shaming
The fat hating, the extra layers of her
The pimple she covers with Shein plastic stickers
In hope that after the darkness it will soon disappear
She doesn't recognise the girl in the mirror
Or even her own family, those telling her she is beautiful
But those words seem so alien, and she understands that isolation
More than that fake-ism that is based on how she looks
Or how she sees herself
The mirror, the glass pieces that speak to her
That gives her daily updates on her weight gain
Sometimes weight loss when she has starved herself
Enough that it shows, and her bones speak
But she still refuses to eat
As she smiles in the mirror.

Memory Loss

Memory loss, they say it's through trauma

that our brain, walls off a memory

Sheltering one from the enemy

that still trying to deplete you of your energy

Memories are fragments of a time that we once lived

Or barely lived but survived, memories that still traumatise

The past of your life that still hurts inside

Like a thousand knives, slicing the scars that slowly healed

Time still reveals it's not always easy to heal

From the mental scars that you cannot see, but hell can you feel

The haunting echoes that still try to climb the very mountains you have built

You are responsible for the torments of her thoughts, and I hope you are burdened with its guilt

For the seconds she struggled to breathe, the minutes she wanted to die, the hours

That tormented her tears and the weeks that made her cry

There are times where these memories flicker like a light-switch

The malfunction of the brain, a memory glitch

Where things start to creep back in, the things you have locked away

That you've hidden out of sight

So, they could never see the light of day

Those damn memories trying to find a way to make you face, what you are trying to forget

Knowing you cannot delete the corrupted files with a reset

Because they are implanted into a field of her

The demons of her memories that no one ever sees

Except the part of her brain that is trying to protect her

With this memory distortion, suppressing the information

That the memories of her past need, to destroy her

To rip apart her organs internally

Memory loss is not always a loss

When it's at the cost of your freedom

Her past thought could mess with her again

But her brain showed her it was the only thing

In place that can ever kill her space

With her past memories

Our bodies work in harmony, to keep us protected

And sometimes our thoughts try to reject this

But she is blessed with, memory distortion.

I cry with you

The brickwork carefully crafted a long line of terraced houses
Perfectly lined together, encased in a world
Where the world knew only of its silence
Nothing of its violence or blunt nails
That clawed at its walls
Leaving bloodied streaks of her screams
Embedded deep into the concrete stone
Pieces of her flesh moulded into the gravel
On the days she tried to escape
the house consumed more of her
More of her tears that strolled down her face
but never created a tsunami
More of her blood that dripped
from her fingertips every time he
barricaded her into the corner of the room
The cold corner, where the damp
wanted to escape as much as she
But there was no escaping her from he
Even her screams stopped at the door
They couldn't forge through the walls
Her body abused, but she was the whore
Living was to earn and to earn was to
See her legs prized open every time
She was pulled from the line
The new virgin bride
Caged in a life of slavery.

The bookstore

Surrounded by religious scriptures, words within pages
The unfamiliar place that should have been filled
With a warm embrace of familiarity
Now was the only comfort and link to becoming halal
In God's eyes and the heart of those who
Couldn't reject that this is where the love lies
To love was forbidden, to be together was a sin
Two lovers wanted to be halal, but no one was listening
They said it was haram to be as one
To want to show each other love
Forbidden to marry without your parents' consent
Even when God himself had sent our souls as one
Two halves of each to represent one whole
Love is not a cultural thing, it's a feeling
It is beyond any human understanding of that meaning
When lovers love and they want to harmonise that love
Without losing God's trust
So, they walk out into an unknown, into a space, a place
Accepted as sin free, to stop the name shaming "haramee"
Together birthed a child out of wedlock
Committing sins daily, she was of a different race
A culture that was too white, and her face
Shone a light that was too bright to be seen clear
His religion sparked a fear, in all whom were dear to her
Two souls alone, two souls that fought to be
The only way they could Islamically
So, they married amongst strangers, amongst books
Witnessed by Allah and his servants
amongst religious scriptures and text
This Is where haram stopped, and Halal met.

Speak your truth

Speak your truth when no one is willing to listen
When you're suffocating with silence
Hold that power and do not give into that resistance
That needs you to be silent in a robotic system
Speak your truth even when you are standing alone
When the chills of wind tries to freeze you
When the storms of the sea try to drown you
When the world is fighting against you
Do not lose you, do not lose you
Keep fighting for truth, speaking your wisdom
Speaking for you, screaming for you
And for the others that will come after you
You leave a trail of speaking your truth
And showing the world that you can stand alone too
And it's one hundred percent the right thing to do
Even when your own heartbeat stays silent
Because it is petrified to beat
Hold your ground, stand firmly and breathe deep
Absorb the Earth from under your feet and take that
Ancestral energy and draw it into you
For the power of truth is you, embodied In Between
The sheet of daylight and last streak of darkness
Cut your losses with those who lost their tongues
When you thought they wouldn't walk, but run to you
Instead, they run from you and watched your soul set ablaze
All the hurt that came your way
But you still Spoke your truth.

Nothing

You are nothing
He keeps her like an ornament sat on the lowest part of his shelf
Collecting dust, and he occasionally allows his breath to blow the growing particles from her face
So, she can too breathe anything other than his breath
Or the collecting dust that sits blocking her airways
She has had enough of his pretence
But she still plays pretend, because
Right now, it is less daunting than thinking of the end
A life without him, she contemplates this path
But allows that freedom to pass
Because she cannot follow a path of uncertainty
 This pain of certainty Is more breathable to live
For he gives her a place standing at the lowest gaze of his
Too much of her is too much for him
But he refuses to let her feel what she is truly missing
He has to keep her, being his property, his walls of brokenness
His cement of unhappiness, his garden of nothing
For she was only every meant to be
 A growing weed that could only be seen
In a garden he controls
Where nothing grows, aligned to two souls that are forced to be together
His energy always over-powering her gentleness
And the wind always reminded her that she too was
A part of the chaos that could live alone
In any thunderstorm, if she believed in her own power
To be as free as she sees in her dreams
And to not stand alone on a bookshelf he created.

The Hand that rocks the cradle

Not once, not twice, too many times
She can't count the amount of signs
That were left ignored
The danger she was running towards
The signs she didn't see
The power and control you had over her
It wasn't the hand she had reached out for
To you, she was a new path to explore
A new piece of land you wanted to conquer
A gentle face that disguised the monster
That you were so intent on hiding
She didn't realise the dangers
Of what you were providing
But your timing was always so perfect
You knew how to manipulate her emotions
Twisting them, then pulling them apart
Rotating them as you tormented her heart
Her knowing she is far from okay
But you, clinging to your sweet words
To make her stay, to stay
In that moment to make you feel wanted
Whilst she felt haunted by your demonic presence
Loving you was her biggest lesson
You had this unhealthy relation going on
And she just couldn't see where she was going wrong
Because it was her that couldn't see
You were mentally unstable
The hand that rocks the cradle was the hand
That was destroying all that everyone else couldn't see.

You Jumped

Always hiding behind the two wrinkled lines that
Deepened as you stretched your smile
Your permanent scars for showing the world
Your heart, for pretending you were happy
You lived a life that most people craved to see
But you never showed them the true reality
You painted your demons as angels
And your heaven seemed beautiful
You fooled us, hiding behind the waves
The stars the moon, the sunset that was truly part of you
But you hid that too
An anchor was pulling down on you
Dragging you to the depths of no return
And you would never come to learn that this,
That the darkness was misguiding you
That, that would pass as seasons pass, as storms brew
The fog that you were fighting through
Would soon clear, and your pathway would
Re-align at just the right time, but time
Was never enough, your thoughts
Drove your demons to light
And you couldn't fight them alone anymore
They told you to jump and usually you'd ignore,
Even laugh at, the voices trying to manipulate your pain
But it became too much, and the blame and the shame
Became too much, it was all too much and the last streak of
Light left when you jumped.

In your eyes

In your eyes lives a thunderstorm that's brewing under a painted rainbow
That God gave you
A dark cloud that clings to a hilly pebbled mountain where the sun appears
to smile just visible amongst the fog that suffocates its wildness
In your eyes there is calmness, a stillness, a gentleness that petrifies
The darkest of demons
There is a fire that burns eternally, burning its own flame repeatedly
Within you, a wildfire sparked from a flicker of your gentleness
That flicker that radiates heat that even the desert quenches its magic
Your eyes speak of all that you do not share and that, that you do
doesn't always reflect the vision everyone else sees
Because no one can dive into your darkness
Into the depth of your ocean, they can barely see the waves
But still craving to be floating, in the ocean they will only down in
Your eyes carry the secrets of your heart and the scars of life
That you will only ever be burdened with and you accept this
Nothing is and will be as it seems
Because not everyone sees with their eyes
They plant seeds of greed within their hearts
And jealousy breeds within their thoughts
Within the walls of their souls
And they lose their power of all they are supposed to control
Because they see and make judgements with their eyes closed
Whilst screaming they are free souls .

Speak for her Sis, Scream for her Sis, Roarrrrrrrr for her Sis

Seek comfort in the wind
Seek Happiness amongst the trees
It's where your happiness lies
And where your future will lead
Stay true to you
Protect all that you are
You are a warrior fighting through
Your battle scars

Can you see?

Can you see, can you see, can you hear, will you listen
Can you see us Pakistani women
Can you see these women that are just not seen
Standing in front of you, but you just see a blank sheet
A question mark that you don't quite understand
Because these women migrated from a different Motherland
They are clothed in light, in rays of pure heavenly wisdom
Stories of life experience, that will never fit into a heartless system
They are the heartbeat that lives in the community, that beats along
Cobbled streets and flows into houses where families meet and greet
and families in time of love and loss is everything
They are the sweet fragrance of spring and the gentle loving arms
That only a mother can bring
Where stories are confined between the walls of their chest
Because grieving seems like its forbidden after death
Losing their loved ones is more than life's challenging test
That one day we will all leave to meet our creator
And the silence that is left is too much to bear
Yet grateful are they for the grief that they share
When the communities come together
When their tears rest upon their scarves
And grief is welcomed by opened arms
From their loved ones, from their neighbours
Help granted by the community strangers
Because in death they grieve as mountains
serving protection to their rainforest and trees
Collectively together, roots standing strong
Knowing that in death the path ahead is lonely and long
But right now, together, together feels strong
And there is a period of time when they face this pain alone

Because the support at the time of death is only shown
For a short period of time and then it's their grief alone
And the silence hits, and the waves of the wind
Rests heavy upon their hearts
and it's not just the grief that wraps around their whole being
it's the financial difficulties when their loved ones depart
So now they are not only feeling the loss of their heart
Their children have to stop education to keep them alive too
And no one sees how the loss of a loved one truly destroys you
And there are places who want to listen, and they deeply want to be heard too
Like they are offered free services of support but without money in
Their pockets to access these services, who's profiting from the support being offered
who are they actually supporting
After the loss of a loved one, these women clothed in Spring
Feel like the whole world is ignoring their pain
and the seasons that change, grief with them
The Autumn leaves are a reminder, that when they wither and fall from the trees
They too will be reborn again in Spring
Hope is always seeing things through Allah's offering
Religion in death and bereavement is everything
For who listens in their silence, in their pain
When darkness falls and they are alone again
In God they seek comfort and comfort he brings
But who other than God is truly listening.

Let go

You know it's time to let him go
You see the warning signs you see the danger
When he's screaming, he hates you
And you stand there and absorb every breath of every
Word, he fires at you
The dagger he stabbed into you, that's still within you
Twisting into your ribs, piercing your oxygen flow
You can barely breathe and the less you breathe feeds his ego
And yet you still believe this is his way of loving you
You are blind to what he is doing to you
Always controlling what you do, who you see
How he manipulates you mentally
And you smile through the tears he creates
As he paints his face with your sadness
You never see how you are destroying yourself to please him
Following him around wherever he goes
And he knows he cages you
You're suffocating while he's breathing
And you still feel you're better off with him than leaving
You think by listening to him, Summer will come sooner
But his garden will never fertilise the seeds that you sow
That you plant into the dirt and want to see grow
Because he doesn't want you to grow, or be known
He doesn't even want you, yet clings to you
Spinning his silken spider-web around you
He sees you as the mud that's embedded into his shoes
After you have scraped the grooves and still a smudge stays
He doesn't love you and will never change his ways
The way he sees you.

Keeping you safe

She tells her to lock the door, make sure the keys are turned at an angle
Anyone knocks just stay quiet and ignore
There is no land to explore or conquer
Keep it locked and bolted always remember
And when you leave the house dear girl
Don't walk with both earphones in
Listen to the howling of the wind
So, you can hear every footstep drawing
Every breath unknowing, stay alert dear girl
Stay alert, and when they scream, 'hey beautiful'
And you want to say 'go screw you'
Instead, you hold your tongue
Because it is safer than putting your life
At danger, my dear girl I salute you
Your patience will guide you
And she hates that she will not always be there to defend you
But she's passed on the skills that will do
Being a girl in a world where men see you
As something sexual, something that pleases their eye
And she wants to rip out their appetite that desires you
Dear girl always remember to look out for you
Look over your left and right shoulder too
And when that last streak of light says goodbye
And it's you and the darkness
Keep your phone alive and keep talking
Make sure you plan the journeys you are walking
Keep safe my dear girl keep safe
And rooooooarrr if you find yourself lost in a place.....
ROARRRRRRRRRRRRRRR.

Blind

Yellow - You gifted her with more than the light that you could ever ignite in the universe
Blue – The ocean waves that are deeply ingrained into her soul, she is grateful for absorbing so much of you into a field of her.
Red - You painted the sky with delicacy that only God's hands could ever create the deepness of red a palette of colour that only our eyes could witness before any hands could re-create.
White – to her you are a vision of purity, a new-born's innocence, white a light that only the moon can ever glorify
Green- How vibrant you are, mountains and everlasting fields how you fulfil her heart
Everything was bathed in light
She lived thinking, that her doctoral degree was her life
Studying from the last streak of light to the darkness that camouflaged the night
Where her soul came alive
It was her dream, her soul calling
That had her smiling every morning
Her eyes would awake and always appreciate
The light that surrounded her soul
Until one day she awoke
 and felt the grief in her throat
She desperately tried to swallow it back in
hold it inside, she screamed she cried
Something inside of her that day had died
and there was nothing she could do
Nothing would ever change the cruel hands of fate
As the dropping of her heart rate, decreased
Her dreams and future beliefs had all been erased

The sadness that's written upon her face
Colours no longer pass her vision, no longer paint her dreams
No sunshine yellow, no ocean blue, no volcanic explosions in the sky
For now, she awakes to the darkness of her eyes
To the darkness of her mind, to the emptiness of her sight
Forever yearning to live to see the daylight, living amongst the blind.

Partition

She laid under your long blood-stained hair that draped over her face
Through the parted strands she could see through
What she could see, she didn't want to see, and she couldn't Even whisper it to you
Your blood stained her clothes that you delicately dressed her in
The streaks of daylight before
Before the screams of partition before the war
She laid there amongst limbs, hands still clutching
Fingertips still touching, arms interlinked
Where the ligaments were ripped apart
Now she sees clearly what once her Mother's Heart was
Is now just a pool of blood attached to her cold body
The warmth of life ripped from her soul, from her being
Fleeing from her ancestral roots
Forced to uproot from her bloodline
Now her mother's body lays intertwined like the whispers
Of grass that flickered through her fingers
When she would dance amongst the fields
Now she lays amongst the still, amongst the silence
Hoping her heartbeat doesn't signal the siren
The war on humanity the violence
She lay counting her breathes, holding one hand on her chest
And the other clenching her lips tight shut
Holding her scream within her, holding her breath
Not knowing how long she too will have left
So, she whispers to herself, "We are going to be okay"
And from moment, from that day, she was the only living human that survived
Every single member of her family had died

And she survived by laying amongst their bodies
Hiding under their limbs, camouflaged by their blood
Now she lives to share her story that no other family
member could.

A Mother's love

You cradled her in your arms, held her close to your skin
Under your rib cage, next to your heart beating, breathing, feeling
She was part of you, and you part of her
Every tiny finger, every hair follicle that curled, she was your baby girl
A daughter who became a mother and a mother who looked on
from afar
Wanting the beat of heart, to sync to the stars
But you were silenced, told not to speak out
Told to bury their abuse, and cloak it under your scarf
And to hold it there, shield it as your veil to protect those
Who would never protect you
You silenced the alarm, preventing any harm from hurting those you
love
To stop the slander of their tongues
Piercing the lungs of those desperately trying to breathe
In the environment they are suffocating from
You swallowed that violence you held it all in
Until the day your heart stopped syncing with her heart beating
The day yours shattered into pieces, scattered across the dust
That lay resting on the side of the pavements
With no possibility of piecing herself back together
She lay under the heavens watching clouds pass over her mother's
grave
Not wanting to leave the land where she grieves
For when she did find the courage to leave
And step back onto UK soil
Her womb was ripped from her uterus with the blood still dripping
Her heart then ripped from her chest
She had just buried her mother now she had to lay her daughter to rest
There is no deeper test than the loss of those who were part of you

Part of your blood, that grew from your cells within you
Nothing prepares you for that pain
Only in God did she find the will to live again.

Fannie Lou Hamer

1961 was the year you surgically removed her womb
You cut at her flesh, cutting away her DNA, her blood, her cells
You gave the portal to her heaven to the dustbins of your hell
You took away more than her own life that day
You severed her attachments to any link of life that was ever destined to be
You forbid her from birthing life, black women were forced to be sterilised
To stop the population of any birth rise
You carved at her, with a butcher's knife
You carved away at her insides
Laying in your hospital amongst your whitewashed walls
And her blood-stained sheets
You scraped and scraped and threw the stands of blood and skin away
And what you set out to destroy created a warrior that day
She changed life for Black women in so many ways
She campaigned and fiercely fought through
Their hands that were all over her, blows to the head, the legs
To her eyes, you made her blind
You took her womb, you took her sight
You couldn't take her voice though you couldn't take her soul
She fought bravely for equality and to stop white control
Yet little do most know of who this phenomenal woman is
Say her name in your classrooms, say her name on the street
Say her name in your workplace, say her name when you sleep
When you sleep soundly for what she did was make history
And set the legacy for everyone else to keep fighting for their
Human right to exist, in a world she wasn't acknowledged
as human.

She (Part 2)

Sometimes, it can be exhausting to speak, to move, to say something positive. To feel alive when you are so busy.

Sometimes, we champion and inspire others to be exactly what you're not yourself, and sometimes, we make a difference without trying.

Sometimes, life can be challenging. We face things and stay silent. Smile and carry on and suffer in silence.
Sometimes, we fight things and hide things and roar at the wind and dance and sing when we are alone.

Sometimes, we are warriors, and sometimes we are like melted chocolate embedded deep into the carpet on the floor, trying to change the liquid mess back whole again.

Sometimes we are magical, with butterfly wings, and we forget everything and just smile.

In the sometimes we fail to recognise how, all the time, we are truly incredible Women

It's easy to forget under the layers of life we live.

How frigging amazing, we are.

Family

It hurt for a moment
Your narcissism was hidden
Her stomach knotted and the gulp
In her throat became harder to swallow
Her gut instinct kicked in
but she chose not to follow
She ignored what her own body had stored
To protect her
Her intuition was howling at her
Pleading please, making her feel this rage
And at this stage she didn't know what to believe
She felt your selfishness it weakened her in seconds
She thought she was stronger than this, she has dealt with much worse life lessons
But here she was, she couldn't ignore
The thunder inside that she refused to let roar
She held it in, she pushed it back down
She roared at herself not to make a sound
Silence was better as she convinced herself
She will always have her own back; she needs nobody else
She spread her arms around her whole being
In hope this feeling would bring her some clarity
But instead, she felt the loss of her
What was happening to her
She felt it, she felt all of your dark energy
Bearing the brunt of your brutality
Born from those you class as family.

Forbidden love

You're the void, the space between now and then

Emptiness, will never mean the same again

Silence, weeps for its secrecy

Regretting the frequency that she ever tuned into

Wishing that station was skipped away from you

Away from the spark

That you ignited in her heart

Away from this feeling, that showed her

What it was like to be human

To lose her senses amongst the confusion

To be free, to think multidimensionally

She hates the pauses, that has her heart

Questioning its own beats

That causes her to feel weak when she breathes

You severed your attachments but

The memory of your love doesn't want to leave

She hates missing you

And you knowing that she does

But you still continue to live life

Like she never mattered

You shattered her heart into pieces

And them scattered them like seeds

That will never blossom, because

The only season they could

Would be a garden, where you stood

Where her roots are fertilised by your soil

But you left that turmoil to her only

Knowing you would leave her lonely

Knowing she was truly alone

Without her only one

Even the dark in the darkness was afraid of her loneliness

Not sure of anything anymore, not sure what to do

Because every silent pause, always leads her back to you

Feeding my soul

I'm trying not to feed into the systematic control

And I'm struggling to feed what aligns my soul

What it yearns, what its hungry for

Them deep conversations, that hold your attention

And fill your soul so much more

Even if it's just me myself and I

Having that moment to, look up at the sky

And stand there, stand as she paints the sky

With her essence, her visible existence means so much

More to me

And I honestly do not know why, I feel so high

In her presence, she captures my attention like

No one ever and I could stand till dawn watching her forever

Till even she,   gets sick of me, wanting her

I just want to lay in a field of wild flowers

Listening to the trickles of water that gently fall

Into each other, droplets embracing one another

I want to lay there for hours, taking goofy selfies

Whilst whispering my secrets to the flowers

I want to be there, right there amongst the fields

of fresh air, standing in the dirt and the mud

its art splashed upon my skin as it should

I miss doing the things that I love

That soothe my sacred feminine spirit

The wind hits differently from the mountain tops

Like it wants to stop, you from pushing forward

Then rewards you for reaching the top

With views that are so hypnotic, orgasmic even

And you can't beat that internal feeling

when you are giving your soul exactly what it's needing

It's times like this, that I miss that feeling.

Grandparents

She is the descendant of a bloodline that intertwines
With different faiths and cultures
Where she once laid as an embryo in her mother's womb,
Where she once laid in her nana's ovaries waiting for her
Roots to be planted, from a cluster of cells to a heart beating
Another life breathing, taking her first breath in
She was the creation born from the ocean and the land
Where sand meets sea but it's not always meant to be
As close as the waves that crash against the rocks
Her mother's father left as quick as the petals on her nana's
Rose stem
Her thorns were not enough to keep away such selfish men
Yet another flower was born from her own mother's thorns
And this flower blossomed was no rose but a wildflower call heather
That grew in the mountain dew and across, windswept hill tops
She was born amongst the UK raindrops and the land in between
the sea
Then there was her, my grandma Bibi whose life was not as free
As a rose growing amongst a thorn bush or a wave crashing in the sea
She was born in a part of the land that caused uproar against man
What once was India is now Pakistan
She left what she once called home, walking miles upon miles
Her body carrying the sheer exhaustion of the tribulations and trials
She had to endure
Leaving her birthland because the rights of man
Where fighting over these lands
And her grandma eventually left to travel over sea
To greet her husband who was working in the UK to help
build their family financially
And here she built her India, with her heavenly scent of

Flowers blossoming and exotic aromas sizzling
And birds always whistling in sync to the early morning sunrise
She was born through two bloodlines, through countries of war
Through separation and borders but what was born through this
Was so much more
A new generation of culture that cannot be divided by borders
Or control
Because they are the children that are born from soul
From the souls of mixed identities
And paths of culture that cross oceans, making waves
Making ripples, bonding cultures together as we should
Celebrating diversity and the stories of her
grandparents' memories from childhood
Because where would we be without them
Without their stories and their past history
She celebrates what makes her different and
What bonds countries, through her grandparent's legacy.

Without me

There is comfort in the warmth of the salt

That once stained her face forcing her eyes to close

Starved of breathing in, what she once let ln

No longer allowing you to impose

Even if she still craves you

Every breath of you

In every moonlit view

She knows she has to let go of things that are connected to you

But try telling that to the water that drenches her skin

Every haunting night

Leaving droplets of you, that swirls through your water supply

Into hers

That leaves her wanting more of you

Leaves her wanting to lay there for hours under the water

That she know travels in ways she never could

In a language that she never understood

Your lips never spoke your secrets

But your eyes always did

What you thought you kept hid

Always found a way to liquidise into her soul

Beyond her blood, way beyond her bones

Every fragment of her, manifested into you

Into this love that she had little or no control of

Yet the seasons of you, consumed her

She could only blossom in your forest

But the wind uprooted her

It changed direction, pushing her onto a path she didn't want to be

And now she is in this life and you're in that life without her

Even the sky paints your name, and the wind screams that you're gone

The breaking of dawn grieves for your light as much as she

And she mourns your existence because goodbye really was goodbye.

Christmas without you

It's time to switch off from the world as most switch on

It's so difficult to celebrate when you're missing what has gone

What is no longer here, and that fear sinks in

You are overcome with that deathly feeling

That longing, that grief

Where pain finds no comfort and is without relief

Where one is hopeless in this darkness

A city filled with festive lights

Leaving this haunting bitterness

Knowing you will not be coming home tonight

Or then again never

Even memories are not promised forever

It's this time of year that seems to attack a little harder

Breaking the pieces of armour, she built to protect

The only piece of her heart that still believes

She can live without you, in this silence without you

In this season that tells her to be happy, embrace the festive cheer

What is to celebrate when you are not near?

And never will be in her physical presence again

So please tell her how can she gift wrap that pain

How can she dress a Christmas tree with tinsel and baubles?
And sit the angel on top, the one that looks down at her
And cannot answer her prayers
But allows her to keep repeating this terrible nightmare
That strikes like dagger at her heart, ripping out
Everything inside
When you left, it wasn't just you who had gone
but everything in her died
so, please tell her how she can celebrate
without you by her side.

Anxiety

Anxiety has been with me for as long as I can remember

Like burning ember that is still glowing after the fire has been extinguished

Just one spark and its rekindled and the damage becomes simple

My hands generate a tsunami of torrential rain from the sweat dripping

off my fingertips

and that's just the start of when anxiety hits, my heart tightens

like someone is gripping it in their hands

and it is getting tighter, and I feel like I have zero chance

at getting through this circumstance that feels like my heart

is being crushed by your hands and broken into pieces

the beating of it increases at lightning speed

and at this stage I'm finding it difficult to breathe

My hands are shaking and I'm weak at the knees

And I'm focusing on just making sure that I can breathe

Because when this happens all, I want to do

Is collapse into a sea of darkness, and hide away

from the world, be invisible, out of sight

for in the darkness, I've always found a way to reach the light

yet in the light I've always felt so vulnerable

Like standing naked in a crowd of people

That fear, that uncomfortable silence

And I hold the space, seeking guidance

From the thoughts that are telling me to just breathe

This moment will pass and leave but I have to proceed

With what I'm doing, I have to overcome that fear

Plant my seeds in that fear, so every root can be born

From that fear, risen from that fear, blossom from that fear

Even if my anxiety doesn't completely disappear

I will keep fighting through fear, through each heart palpitation

Through every complication I will break free

From the chains that keep haunting me,

I will not allow Anxiety to keep crippling me

Back into my comfort zone.

My silence

It whispers to you, like the wind gently whispers to the rain

You feel the depth of me to the very root of my pain

You feel me without feeling me, you know

Exactly at which moment the heart rate grows

Because you know me and you know my silence

The silent pauses, the long deep breaths, the longing

In the silence is a warm place of belonging

A home crafted by your hands, carved by your fingertips

My love sits in our silence, in the awkward pauses

In the ocean stare, it's right there

In them waves that crash against your heart

That you feel what I feel, when your heart beats

When it races at speed

That attacks how you breathe

Because every breath that you leave

Wants us to be, the very breath in between

Your heartbeat and my waves of energy

Our love manifests from the silent tests

That we are forced to face at times

When we deeply crave to communicate

Not even the hands of fate can stop this alignment

It's in them moments of silence

That I feel you, like I hear you

In your silence we communicate in ways

That has our heart rate, pulsing and breathing

And believing that this sacred feeling can only ever

Join souls that were together, way before life existed

on this universe

Only here on this Earth, did we feel this human connection

For you know me, you know me beyond this human form

Only with your silence did it soothe the storm within me

You know me.

Write

I want to write all my heart's secrets and pour them out to the universe

Share some of that happiness and burden the earth with my pain

What if I could plant it in the dirt, would flowers eventually blossom in the rain

What if weeds grew too and the fine dandelion seeds blew my dreams

Into reality, what if I stopped all that I'm doing right now

Would I be happier somehow, or would I regret giving up

When it's never been an option for me. yet sometimes

The things we give up allow more than our spirit to be free

And sometimes that's exactly what I need for me

To have the days where it's just me myself and I

To bathe in the whole ocean and wrap the warmth of the sky

Around my whole being, if only it's me seeing the waves that I'm swimming

I want to pause the life that I'm living for even just few minutes a day

To check to see if I'm doing okay because I sometimes lose my way

When I'm focusing on others but forgetting that I exist too

Because it's so easy to do, and you have to check up on you

I wish I could sometimes scream what I knew, the thoughts inside

That I have to hide because of the experiences in life that

Others have put me through

You know those smiles that disguised the lies

When people want to extract the fragrance of your essence

In a bottle they contained and call their own

And I smiled and allowed it because whatever will grow

Will be grown with the seeds that I've sown

With this heart of my own, and if the lies are never shown

That fragrance will always be part of my own

Even if nobody ever comes to know, I know

And my creator does too, and ill humbly stay silent

So, you can roar that the ideas were from you

So here I am, writing the findings that I try to suppress

It's time to tidy up this mess that's being growing cobwebs

In the corridors of my mind

It's time to sweep it clean and find the exit

Cleansing my soul from the times I've been desperate

Wanting to become reckless, It sometimes takes time

To come to your senses

And when you do

Just know that nothing in this life is ever going to stop you

The only person that can do that will only ever be you

So never keep fighting your corner for you.

I'm helpless in Helping you

I'm helpless in helping you,

I wish I could fight the darkness for you

There are so many things I crave to do

But I'm helpless, helpless in helping you

And I wish I could escape you from you

From the darkness, from the deep aches that

Suffocate your every positive thought

I wish I could do more, I want too

I want to be right there with you

I want to crawl into your thoughts and tell them

who do they think they are trying to weaken

You are not just part of Spring but needed in every season

In ever Sunset, in every downpour of rain

You're needed, but how can I tell that to your brain

When it's telling you, you're better off dead

And you're thinking it's easier because

you cannot process what's going on in your head

and I know you're trying and it's that, that kills me inside too

I didn't think I'd see the day, when I'd be sat here missing you

Because you were always the tornado, the lightning strike

Two bodies that were different, two souls that were alike

You were the strong one, the so what, fuck it one

The dancing on cars, and you told me never to hide

My battle scars, because that pain could only dissect my heart

If I allowed too,

You tell me every time when I see you, that I'm beautiful,

Because you know I don't see me as beautiful

Yet u do, and you make me fully aware of it too

And I,   I just Love you

and I'm sorry I'm helpless in helping you

I'm sorry that I cannot be your shelter from

The floods that you create

I want to call upon the wind to ease your heart rate

To wrap around your whole being

So you can feel, what you're not seeing

I want to help you; I wish I could help you

In helping you, in helping yourself

To bring you back from the prison

Of your own mental health

But for now, I'll have to wait

and sit with you in the darkness

I'll be the moon outside your window

I'll be feathers that capture your tears on your pillow

And I'll never let go, or let you let go

Of that rope

Even if I'm helpless, in helping you cope

I'll stay helpless for one day you will come to know

How much, how much I miss you

I'm helpless in helping you

What is happiness

Happiness is writing poetry at midnight when the sky wraps its darkness.

around my whole being, it's listening to rain, to mother nature playing

to her whispering that another day is awaiting

and if this day was not what I expected to be facing then

tomorrow is another day awaiting, another day to replace things

To re arrange and adjust, to change (deep) Breath in)

Happiness is just that, the pause in between, that deep breath in

It's the breathing, it's appreciating that as you take that deep breath in

Someone on this Earth is leaving

Taking their last, happiness is right now

It's looking around at all that surrounds you and being grateful for it too

To look to see, to create a living memory of that you're looking at

Happiness is sometimes looking back, because not all memories

Are full of crap, some are delicately beautiful

Happiness is sitting under a full moon, as the candlelight flickers

Halos on my bedroom walls

Watching the shadows fall into each other

Dancing in sync to the silence

Happiness is nature's guidance, how it makes me feel worthy

Of being in its presence, like I'm fully accepted for being me

My flaws and my imperfections that everyone says they don't see

But I do, and it sometimes really kills the inside of me too

It's still an ongoing battle that I continue to fight

I know happiness is not always about looking perfectly right

In everyone else's eyes, it's about you feeling perfectly right for you

And sometimes I feel amazing too and it's them days that I know

I have to hold on tightly, to pull myself through

And I do, I get to the place were selfies

Are taken and I share the fake smile on my face

Well sometimes it's real, and the times the selfie never captures

It's always real, I'm too busy smiling to capture that is real

To show the world how it feels, because I'm too busy feeling it

Absorbing that shit, that happiness that hits

Happiness is not always captured in a picture, it's captured in your heart

It's everything that gives you that feeling that inner meaning

Like oooof this feels damn good and it's a feeling that can be misunderstood

When you don't fully accept its truth

Happiness is more than you show and it's more than I ever show to a cold-hearted world

Where people hate to see you happy. So, I stay authentically me and the world only gets to see

What I choose to show.

Do you have moments?

Do you have moments that release

Where you want to be loved, and loved

And hugged and touched

So much, where warm arms embrace

Around your waist

And you're held there

In that silence in that space

Is the days you crave to be touched?

To be wanted, to tattoo where you were last kissed

Do you ever miss his hands on your skin?

That release that sensual feeling

That gentle kind of loving that patient kind of knowing

That compassion, he is   showing

That delicate kind of loving where

Two eyes cross rivers and oceans

Sailing into a bed of emotion with just one glance

Do you have moments that stop them moments?

*

And in that moment, you wish to be alone

To be miles away from home

To be on your own, to listen to the wind and rain pour

To listen to the howling of sea splashing against the shore

It's easier to ignore what you are trying to escape

Because when you're alone no demon can take shape

And many hate that ignorance that is crucial to your existence

Because sometimes, alone time is what I crave the most

To be loved and to be alone, you cannot diagnose

That weirdness, and I cannot explain why

At sometimes I love your nearness

And at others I crave your disappearance

Do you ever have moments like this?

Me, myself and my poetry

I've been feeling a little low
So I'm writing this poem as I go
Well I'm not going anywhere
I'm actually sat in the bath with
Bubbles overflowing
Somehow the gurgling noise of water eases my anxiety that is growing
That is clouding my thoughts but not allowing the rain to release
I'm trapped temporarily in its storm
And I know it will pass it always does
But the pain always tragically seems to last
Beyond its expiry date
If only it had an expiry date
Like I wish I could be vocal about the silent hate
I preach to others, like the blue streaks that stretch across the sky endlessly
about amplifying your own voice
Yet I silence my own
Because I stand alone, in every crowded building in every busy filled street
It's just me, it seems like it's just me
Because it's just me
And people's cold actions mess with my insecurities
That most think I shouldn't have
And I do and it separates my chest from my heart too
And it grips it tight, telling me it's my fault for being too nice
For being too over polite
for caring for trying to make a difference
In a world that runs a soulless system

A society that cares only for what you can offer or what others can steal
Even your closest these days are not even real
But then again when was they ever
Just a ticked box in most people's lives and not seen as human so an easy sacrifice
And know this will only make sense to me and each line still holds a message subliminally
To protect others that would never protect me
And thank you for allowing me to breathe
To word release once again
This crippling pain, you always have a way of saving me
It's always
Me, myself and my poetry.

Different

Am I so different to you?

Why does this hate breed?

From an implanted seed that I never planted

Why do your eyes

Look at me with hatred,

That you try to disguise

But your body language shows me so clearly

That you don't want to be near me

Am I so different to you that you choose to hate

To fuel and discriminate

Do you see this as acceptable behaviour?

Instead of fuelling hate

We could be the generation, to make this world greater

Be the change of past history and start learning from our

Neighbours

Why do you hate me, why are you threatened by the layers of my skin?

That shines in a different shade to you

Yet within, our internal system is the same

Our blood flows like identical twins and our bodies are clothed

With the keystrokes of our identity

Why am I, seen as the enemy?

Labelled into categories that seem less discriminating

So, people feel comfortable in communicating

But that's not stopped People from hating

Because different is different in societies system

I'll always fall victim to this hate

To this untreated disease

That feeds the ignorant

Yet I'm hopeful that there will be a cure

To this hate that sees me as different.

The Light of the Lantern

The waves of darkness never brought the light of the lantern
The promise land was always the broken promise of the sea
Young marriages of just thirteen, living under the halo of the lanterns
And limited electricity
We lived under an endless sky, where walls never contained our cries
For our homes in our homeland were as free as the butterflies
That fluttered their wings amongst the wind
Our homes were the sky, they were the sea, they were everything
That represented a land that was free
Our Motherland was the heart of me and here we were
In a land that's dark and empty craving the warmth
Of the lanterns, even a flicker of candlelight
Would have warmed the waves of darkness
That had us craving the rays of the sunlight
Missing the morning sunrise
Missing the sweet fragrance of home
Stuck In between the cement and the stone of these brick walls
That separate us from our sky from our sea
From the loving arms of home country
Living in the dreamland, wasn't what we thought it would be
We missed the heat that painted our faces every morning
We missed the open streets, the landscape
The disappointment of darkness that began to suffocate
Our hearts when we remembered the light of the lanterns
The home of our Motherland, the home of our hearts
That we had to migrate, our bodies left but our souls never did depart
Even the soles of our feet left a piece of us there
Embedded into the soil, weaved into the grass
Our eyes, still part of the windowpane and clear-cut glass
Our memories are still alive in every golden lantern lit

In every flicker of that flame
Oh, those days, the old days that the darkness always over came.

(With thanks to Women Zone ladies and Maya Productions for this piece would have never been written without you)

Saying no

She lived thinking that every opportunity
Was an opportunity to grow
Saying yes too many times when the answer should have been no
It took her several years to realise
That not everyone wants to see you grow
Your ambition and drive will storm crash
Their sky, because not everyone wants to
See you spread your wings and fly
Her heart was too open, delicately fragile
Like a bookshelf with books left opened
Her knowledge and pages is what she shared with all she had spoken
Life was about giving, giving more than she could ever receive
Uplifting others so they never forgot how to believe
In themselves in their abilities and how to achieve, in all that they
thought was nothing more than a dream
Her success was seeing others changing their reality
Not everyone would share this knowledge for free
Vultures and prying eyes are always ready to attack when it involves
making money
Whilst harvesting the new nests born but seen as an idol publicly
Life as a poet is not always what it seems
Everyone seen her living the dream
All her success is what most wanted to devour
Years and years of spreading her seeds,
All the blood sweat and tears of this wildflower
Not once ever seen the endless rejection
That made her believe she was forever destined
Always questioning, the endless no sorry it's not right for us, not
enough experience for us
Sorry, who are you again?

Having to explain that she's just a poet
Living in their doubt, she was made for great things She just
didn't know it
It's not always easy to believe in yourself
And that negativity can really impact your health
That feeling of not being good enough
For society's expectations
When did being creative ever come with a label
Bios become your public ego to feed to a society
That you are expected to show
Your long-listed achievements before you have had
the opportunity to grow
How much I have despised those bios
Some opportunities need to be greeted with no
Not every opportunity is an opportunity
To be planted.

Now Roarrrrrrrrrrrrrrrrrrrrrrrrrrrrrrrrrrrrrr

Roar with me

Break the Bias

Today I ask you to pause for a moment, to look within

Look deeper within, beyond the surface of the largest organ of your body, beyond the skin

I want you to look at how you think, how you process

Your thoughts, where you filter what you think

It's there, where you need to break the bias and consciously break the link

I want to say I stand for equality, but equality has never been fair to us

You see, where always less than enough, when it comes to a male dominated world

No woman or girl, is ever equally represented

Unless it's on your tv screens or social media feeds

Where a woman's face needs to be seen

For ratings to increase or a new beauty product released

It's time to break the bias, to stop those false advertisements

Create new feminine alignments, our own tables that we are not climbing

To Climb in, to sit waiting upon the ladder till it's the right timing

We will not be the checklist ticked, in your boxes that are fixed

So you appear to be covering equality grounds to gain funding

Whilst we temporally sit at your table

When we are more capable of creating tables that do not discriminate

against gender, disability nor ethnicity, religion, or hate or to fill your ticked boxes

Why is it that ticked boxes are there, so people have to play fair, so it's logged down and seen,

Behind the screens we don't see

shouldn't it always be consciously there without being the tick on the check list

It's right here where you need to stop and consciously think

Let this sink deep into your thought process

What are you doing to break the bias

What are doing to stop the injustice, when a woman or girl is seen as too much

Too bold as such, judged by the colour of her skin for being too overpowering

When showering her voice against the thunder that roars

That echoes that screams, and all one can ever see is the misconceived perception

Making judgements when you have never tasted discrimination or hate

Never felt the fire burn in your soul when every pathway is another locked gate

Because your seen as different, and different is always attached to reactions

With no justifications for one's actions, for one's cold response

Different

We are women of different seasons, winter and some dancing into spring,

Flowers unapologetically blossoming, in the gardens we choose to grow

The only differences that divide us, is the ignorance & hate that people show

We are one of the same, roots that grow from decades of ancestral generations

Weaved together through stands of women that live amongst us and those

Who have travelled through the puddles of their own tears and separation

We have to break the bias, so no more generations have to face the brutality of discrimination

We have to be the voice of reason, the action of change

Breaking the chains so no woman or girl has to suffer in the injustice of this world

We have to break the bias, what are you doing to break the bias

What are you doing?

In memory of every woman who has fought for us, spoke out for us, be the change for us, empowered us. For all the women that cannot be with us, your memory lives on within us.

DEEDS NOT WORDS IWD

Seen as the weaker sex, too many emotions, too many hormones, too many feelings
Women seen as either too fragile or over appealing
We are nature's medicine the all healing
The gentle dew drops that Mother Nature scatters amongst her soil
We spread our seeds, and sprinkle life into those dandelions that you call weeds
Creating life, creating peace, we live and breathe
On this Earth, and we are the ones whose bodies
Breathe life into one's soul when they give birth
When her body nurtures and protects the life inside
No one ever sees, the pain she endured or the tears she cried
When the morning sickness erupted every, morning noon and night
Her body adapted and she gave up her appetite
She gave in to the cravings that helped this little life grow
This deep embedded embryo that will eventually grow
We was given the power to birth life and we always seem to sacrifice
Our own life to see others thrive and blossom in their own
Women over the generations have shown
Their strength and determination fighting for our rights
With Emmeline Pankhurst always the first to fight, for women's rights
We have to keep voicing our voice, deeds not words
Roaring like lions instead of tweeting like birds
Women are more than just female, they are deep rooted to the core
To earth to the ground the whistling in the breeze that creates its own sound
We are fire, the very flames that burn, we ignite, and we spark that light
We are water as pure as it falls, we pool oceans and waves

Planting memories of life and forgetting how quick the days
Fall into each other, we are the children of all mothers
Of all women and men, it's us women that breathe life into spring all over again
It's women that are child bearing, the all daring, the all loving the all caring
It's women that carry on selflessly, that nurture our very lands
With arms and open hands and strive for strange
For equality, for respect, to fight child abuse and neglect, and we do this for voices of women lost in silence
Women who are trapped in domestic violence
We do this to stop rape, to stop war to stop racial discrimination and so much more
We do this for the women and girls now and for the women who came before
We will never ignore the message and we will continue to proceed.

Faces of the present Iwd 2021

We are the faces of the present
Different phases like the full moon, like Lunas crescent
That divine link to the Earth and the heavens
We are the descendants of the Women that came before us
Of future generations that are yet to be born
The birth before the storm, before the wild wind breathes
Into a life that, believes in her warrior soul
We are leaders, Leaders of love and compassion
Of freedom and self-expression
We are the women that stand firmly against oppression
Seeking Justice and equality in all that we do
Raising our voices so that all women's voices are heard too
Shattering that silence, that deathly silence
With every breath that we breath and every Echo
We scream, we will not allow women to suffer at the hands
Of violence, at the hands of any abuse
Or to be used and seen as the weaker sex
We are not objects, we are life, we hold the divine universal power
We are waves, waves that ripple in every ocean
And every ripple that rings, expands into the sea

Creating this universal energy, that's beyond any human being

It's a sisterhood, it's a connection that can only ever be understood

By she, by her, by me by understanding that once one woman

Stands her ground, raising the volume and speaking loud

Her voice travels through whispers of fine bladed grass

Through the thick fog that sweeps across mountain tops and crashes against the raging sea

Her voice is the very heartbeat that bonds hearts of unity

We are the faces of women that stand proudly together

To be the change we want to see, for every woman to be heard

Raise your voice, as I've done mine, so no women's voice goes ever Unheard.

Embrace Equity

We are one
We enter life from a tunnel of Silence
Of Darkness
Leaving the comfort of our mother's wombs
Our screams of Innocence that fill the walls of our birth room
We are born into a world from the same portal of life
And no life is more alive than any life that is born
We are born as naked as our souls
As pure as our hearts
As innocent as our screams
So why are the lives of some branded and seen
As more or less of a human being
Than any other life
From innocence we are born
We are the seed from one root that grows
In different directions
Dancing in different seasons
Seasoned by the environment we thrive in
Or hide in
Not feeling appreciated at the tables we are trying to survive in
Brown eyes should be looked upon the same as one's blue
And one's blue shouldn't reflect that two colours effect
How the two of us are viewed
Our skin shouldn't be a portal to a checklist
That fits a failing system
But a system that sees through
In between the cracks of how marginalized and unrepresented
Some are forced to live through
Equity starts With me
And with you

Challenging the wrong
And following it right through
Equality has to start grounded from our roots
The soil we live in has to be soil we weave our dreams into
Our voices have to be the voice of reason
In every breath we breathe in
In every strand of light, weaved into every morning of every season
We have to all come together to embrace the change
To eradicate the hate
The inequality that plays
In a system we want to change
It starts with us
With showing kindness and love
That love that comes from within
If we can feel it
We can breathe it
It can pour from our energy like waves of electricity
To erase any discrimination or toxicity
We can do this
We have got this
Together we can fight this
And embrace the arms of equity
Working collectively
As one.

THE END OF THE BEGINNING

If you have reached here, thank you. Thank you for reading my soul into yours and that of the women's voices that go unheard the poems that I felt I needed to share. I know it's not been easy, and this journey has taught me a lot. I was given this chance, maybe it was fate, it most definitely was destiny, and it wouldn't have ever being created I don't think, if it wasn't Thanks to Ace for gifting me the time, I needed to develop this book. I initially had this idea of going back to my past to share the experiences that I felt ready to express. Poetry has always been a form of healing for me, and I wanted to express the memories in my thoughts that once use to haunt me. I wanted to empower myself by exposing my own demons and showing the world that we can heal our hurt. I didn't realise when I first started writing this book how difficult that would be, I had to re visit fragments of a time that still painfully lingered in the back of mind somewhere. I had to pull them to surface and sit with them feelings, sit, and watch the younger me. How she dealt so fiercely with everything that was set out to destroy her. I thought writing this book would be easy, pain and poetry always seemed to go hand in hand, yet my brain decided "Memory distortion was better for me" some memories are locked away for a reason, a triggered from of amnesia. I realised I was clinging on to a thought of a memory that no longer affected me because as I went in deeper it had been erased from the place it once poisoned. In this book you will have found pieces of me, pieces of other women's experiences, maybe you heard your own voice too. I truly believe in the power of poetry, and I believe it from the depths of my heart, because poetry has a way of changing lives. It helped me find the strength to change mine, and now it still runs through my veins in all that do. As I'm sat writing you, as you're reading me.

Poetry is me, a beacon of light that set me free and I am honoured to have shared the poems I have shared in this book, some of the poems inspired by incredibly brave women and their experiences that humble me, that made me so grateful to be alive. To be able to breathe, to use my eyes to see.

Writing this book taught me so much, poetry cannot be rushed, revisiting past times you can find yourself at a wall, that is higher than any mountain, with the sun shining over and daisies chained delicately together. warning you not to break the seal but stand enjoy the sunshine, we are not meant to revisit past times. Writing this book has taught me, we can start out on a journey with a clear intention in our mind, but paths change course, and there are bumps in the road and sometimes puddles too and we have to change our route. It's all about learning. The path is our teacher, the journey is our guide. We have to keep on learning and some changes we have to sacrifice but we have to keep going, we have to keep speaking our truth, speaking our times, speaking what's wrong against what others say is right. Poetry is the truth that will break down any lie and It enters hearts like no lover could pierce. I wanted to make sure I continued She's journey (My first book) as she is very much part of me and my river flow of life. So, I too hope you too enjoy those poems. Keep speaking your truth and thank you for believing in mine.

THANK-YOUS

First and foremost, I thank my creator Allah Swt for gifting me life, I once cursed the universe for my existence for the struggles, the challenges the pain. Now everything makes sense and patience has taught me so much, my faith has kept me strong, it has kept me motivated and my heart grateful for every breath that I have breathed in, even at the times I wanted to pause that very breath from leaving my body, from escaping me I am thankful. Alhamdulliah for everything.

I thank my Mum; she taught me that I am a warrior and that I can defeat anything that comes at me if I believe in myself. I broke the link, I severed its attachments, and I forgave, for heaven lies under my mother's feet and my path may not be in sync to hers but I pray for her always and I will love her always, from daughter to Mother, I will be forever grateful of this life you gifted me.

To my Husband to my girls

My Triple A team, I have been gifted with the best gift of life that one could be granted. My beautiful wildflowers that are my biggest blessing. I love you all so very much and I thank you for your patience, for the times Mum Is busy writing, working, travelling, attending events. I do it all for us and you know this too and as you watch me grow; I watch the growth it inspires in all three of you. The independence it creates, the fierceness to challenge the wrong, the love it generates that keeps your soft hearts wrapped in layers of the universe, sprinkling your beautiful energy like stars across the sky. I am one super proud Mum and grateful for all that I am blessed with, to my husband thank you for every minute of every day for believing me, encouraging me, supporting me and allowing me to become the butterfly I needed to be with your support and love.

My Sisters, Tanya & Marcia – blood sisters, birth sisters, soul sisters, you taught me how to survive, you were my mum and my light, you taught me how to fight for me, to live for me. You don't realise how watching you fight to live, made me fight to live too. How watching you breastfeed your kids, made me want too, too. We all turned out alright in the end, and I have nothing but love for you two.

My baby Sister Natasha – you make me so proud watching you live your dreams, authentically true to you. Living your life and taking steps that most dream. I've watched you grow from a delicate flower to a strong, independent fierce, beautiful Lioness. Thank you for being my baby sister.

To my brothers. I love you all so much, I cannot thank you enough, and I cannot write what I am trying to explain I am so grateful for, but you know. You know your sisters struggles and her heart very well.

To my Dad ~ I am glad you broke free from all that prevented us being close, ive watched your closet leave this life and with them a huge part of you left too. Yet you still continue to be my good morning sunshine. Thank you.

My Sis in law Rabeeya ~ Your strength and determination inspire me, your kindness, your love has meant everything to me, and if anyone could ever understand my Anxiety, you could, you understand me. You make me so proud, you're such a beautiful beautiful human being. I am so proud of you.
To my family, thank you for believing in me, loving me, having faith in me. I love you all

I want to thank The Verve Poetry Press for believing in me, and showing me that every rejection I faced, happened because here and now is my destiny. My work is seen across rivers and seas because they believed in my work, the vision I dreamed became my reality.

I thank Dionne V Hood at Bradford libraries for everything she has helped me with, supported me with. I can't thank this lady enough. As a poet I cannot even describe how incredible she is and how she has supported me throughout my poetry journey from day one. She is a role model, a mentor amazing human being and a woman whom I truly admire. Thank you, Dionne, for everything.

I want to wish my friend Suhaiymah Manzoor Kahn for reading you before anyone else did, for gifting me your time and your wisdom. I admire all that you do, thank you.

I thank all my friends, my poetry family, Sisterhood family, Bajis on Brighton beach, everyone who has supported me. I have nothing but love for you all.

Abda, Sonia, Fran, Jodie, Asma, Saima, Neelofer, Yvonne, Susan, Fehmida, Sarah, Shamim, Jenny, Laura, Zara, Rose, Claire, Pauline, Zoe, Gemma, Amria, Sarah, Reyhana, Halima, Barbara,, Dex, Geraldine, Ella, Jamila, Lence, Eileen, Rubina, Margaret, Andrew, Farah, Kayleigh, Fiona, Courtney, John, Uzma, Vie, David, Jamie, Daniel, Luca, Peter, Jill and Kevin, Becky, Michelle, Cathryn, Luke, Kieron, Amanda, Scott, Graham, Izzy, Sophie, Mati, Kerry, Matt, Aaminah, Fiona, Paula, and everyone else who has impacted my life in some way, with your kindness, your belief in me. Thank you.

Jess ~ Shine bright beautiful Earth Angel, you are missed.

Bradford Libraries, The Leap, Kala Sangam, Women Zone, Maya Productions, Huddersfield Lit festival, Laurence Batley Theatre, Bradford Literature festival, The Sisterhood beauty bar, National Literacy Trust, Blur the Lines. and the list goes on.......

Let's always rise together Sisters

We are women that want to be heard
We wish for a space which is safe for us women to spread our word

~Sonia Kauser

Empower me with devotion, a raw emotion of purity
Sanity is controlled by dietes, reality hits my femininity
Is it your responsibility or mine to fall within society

~Jodie

Roadmap
My body is a roadmap
Every winding Road
Tells the story of a time
I carried a heavy load.

~Laura J Baldwin

I was still in the womb
when I learnt to tell the truth, and I've walked in my truth ever since.
Finding my voice in truth has been the most powerful gift I could ever give to the voiceless.

~Neelofer Nova Poetry 2023

Every leaf has its own colour and shape
Colours are the narrative of the story
The Journey of a beginning not an end

~Rubina warsi

Jigsaws of old
I puzzle at the complexity
I find my daughters in
I pray for simplicity
I am satisfied with contentment
I find it endlessly in supply

~ Asma Malik

As I stand here in your back garden, fists clenched, jaw right,
Red stripes leaking from my face and dirty from the fight.
All I want to do is change the perspectives of society that we are not crazy,
We are just wired differently. Will you love me then?

~Courtney Ward

Ya Ummi you have a beautiful heart
Always full of dua's when we meet and when we depart
May Allah ﷻ enter happiness upon your heart, as you enter happiness upon ours
And may Allah ﷻ feed you the best foods from Jannah and may you sit amongst Jannahs flowers

~Saeema Majid

With love they write
With hate they write
With sorrow they write
With the ink of my soul I'll write

~ Farah Nazley

ALSO AVAILABLE FROM VERVEPOETRYPRESS.COM

Eighty Four:
Poems on Male Suicide, Vulnerability, Grief and Hope

With an introduction from editor Helen Calcutt

Eighty Four was originally a new anthology of poetry on the subject of male suicide in aid of CALM. Poems were donated to the collection by Andrew McMillan, Salena Godden, Anthony Anaxogorou, Katrina Naomi, Ian Patterson, Caroline Smith, Carrie Etter, Peter Raynard, Joelle Taylor, while a submissions window yielded many excellent poems on the subject from hitherto unknown poets we are thrilled to have been made aware of.

We hope this book will shed light on an issue that is cast in shadow, and which is often shrouded in secrecy and denial. If we don't talk, we don't heal and we don't change. In Eighty Four we are all talking. Are you listening?

Available in paperback:
ISBN: 978 1 912565 13 9
188 pages • 216 x 138 • 56 poems
£11.99

And on eBook:
ISBN: 978 1 912565 79 5
£6.99

ALSO AVAILABLE FROM VERVEPOETRYPRESS.COM

Postcolonial Banter
Suhaiymah Manzoor-Khan

The bestselling debut collection from this powerhouse of poetry!

Postcolonial Banter is Suhaiymah's debut collection. It features some of her most well-known and widely performed poems as well as some never-seen-before material. Her words are a disruption of comfort, a call to action, a redistribution of knowledge and an outpouring of dissent.

Ranging from critiquing racism, systemic Islamophobia, the function of the nation-state and rejecting secularist visions of identity, to reflecting on the difficulty of writing and penning responses to conversations she wishes she'd had; Suhaiymah's debut collection is ready and raring to enter the world.

Available in paperback:
ISBN: 978 1 912565 24 5
88 pages • 216 x 168 • 28 poems
£10.99

And on eBook:
ISBN: 978 1 912565 78 8
£7.49

ABOUT VERVE POETRY PRESS

Verve Poetry Press is an award-winning press that focused initially on meeting a local need in Birmingham - a need for the vibrant poetry scene here in Brum to find a way to present itself to the poetry world via publication. Co-founded by Stuart Bartholomew and Amerah Saleh, it now publishes poets from all corners of the UK - poets that speak to the city's varied and energetic qualities and will contribute to its many poetic stories.

Added to this is a colourful pamphlet series, many featuring poets who have performed at our sister festival - and a poetry show series which captures the magic of longer poetry performance pieces by festival alumni such as Polarbear, Matt Abbott and Imogen Stirling.

The press has been voted Most Innovative Publisher at the Saboteur Awards, and has won the Publisher's Award for Poetry Pamphlets at the Michael Marks Awards.

Like the festival, we strive to think about poetry in inclusive ways and embrace the multiplicity of approaches towards this glorious art.

www.vervepoetrypress.com
@VervePoetryPres
mail@vervepoetrypress.com